Scales and Tails

Klay Lamprell

BARNES
& NOBLE
BOOKS

NEW YORK

This 2005 edition published by
Barnes & Noble Publishing, Inc.,
by arrangement with Fog City Press.

Barnes & Noble Publishing, Inc.
122 Fifth Avenue
New York, NY 10011

ISBN 0-7607-6714-9

Printed and bound by SNP Leefung in China

05 06 07 08 09 MCH 10 9 8 7 6 5 4 3 2 1

Contents

Looking at Scaly Things

Scales are hard pieces of skin, like fingernails, which cover the bodies of many creatures. Most scaly creatures, such as fish, snakes, lizards, turtles and crocodiles, are cold-blooded animals. Mammals are warm-blooded. Some, such as mice and opossums, have scaly tails. Only one mammal, the pangolin, has scales on its body. The shape and size of a creature's scales give clues to where it lives, what it eats and what it is eaten by.

▲ The scales on a fish are loosely attached, and can come off.

4

Which scaly creatures here are cold-blooded?

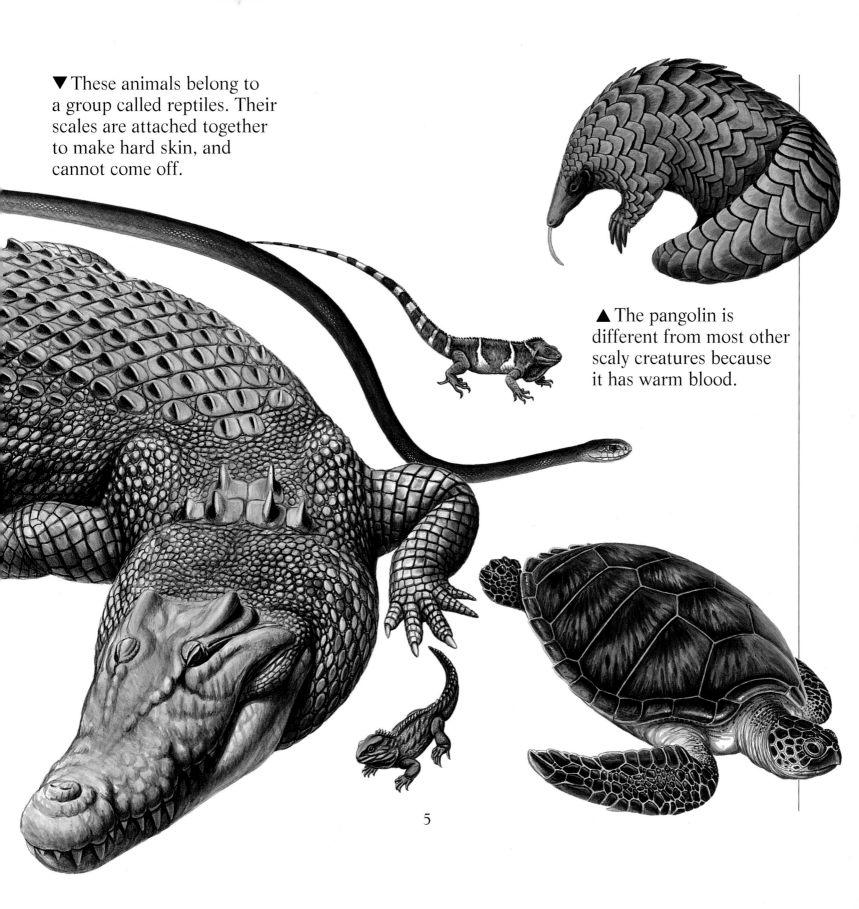

▼ These animals belong to a group called reptiles. Their scales are attached together to make hard skin, and cannot come off.

▲ The pangolin is different from most other scaly creatures because it has warm blood.

5

Slow and Steady

What shapes can you see in this tortoise's shell?

Turtles have scales on all parts of their bodies, even on their bony shells. Turtles that live on land, called tortoises, mostly have shells that are high and round. They can pull their head and tail inside the shell to hide from enemies. The shells are very heavy, which is one reason tortoises move so slowly. They eat things that also move slowly, like snails, or things that do not move at all, like plants. Some turtles can stay alive for months without food.

◄ The Galápagos Islands tortoise is enormous compared to the South American red-footed tortoise and the tiny spider tortoise.

▶ This tortoise shell is empty. Tortoises cannot crawl out of their shells, which are their skeletons.

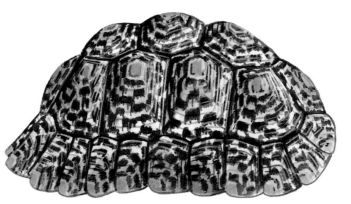

▼ Tortoise legs have claws for walking and digging.

◀ This radiated tortoise, from the island of Madagascar, could live to be more than 100 years old.

▲ A sea turtle's leg is like a flipper. Freshwater turtles have webbed toes to help them walk on land.

Sea turtles can

Scaly Flippers

Two kinds of turtles live in water—freshwater turtles and sea turtles. Most freshwater turtles go onto land often. Most sea turtles go ashore only to lay eggs. The shells of turtles that live in water are flat and light so that they can swim easily and catch fish and water insects to eat. Like land tortoises, water turtles have no teeth. They grind their food with sharp-edged beaks.

Why do freshwater turtles have toes?

◀ Like most female sea turtles, the green sea turtle comes ashore once a year to lay her eggs at the beach where she hatched.

swim as fast as humans run

◀ The shells of Pacific hawksbill turtles were once made into combs and jewelry.

Sit and Wait

Crocodiles and alligators are part of a group called the crocodilians. This group also includes caimans and gharials. Crocodilians live in and near water, in very warm places. Their eyes and nostrils are set high up on their heads so they can hide underwater but still see out and breathe. They wait for their prey to come close and then pounce. Because their teeth can only grip, not chew, crocodilians swallow small prey whole, or twist and shake large prey until it breaks into pieces.

10

Crocodiles can be four times as long as an adult human.

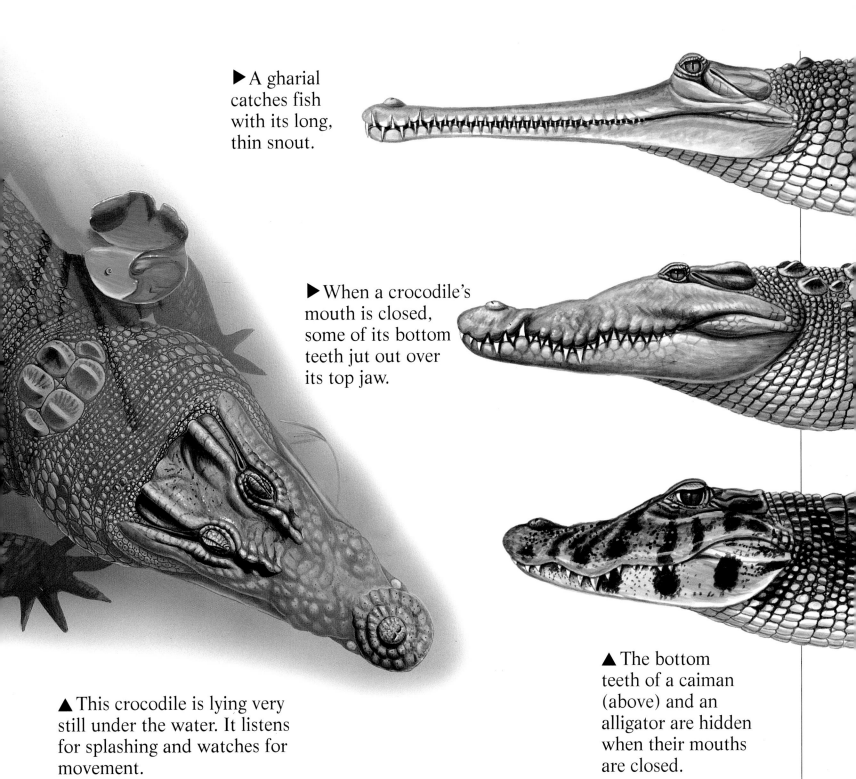

▶ A gharial catches fish with its long, thin snout.

▶ When a crocodile's mouth is closed, some of its bottom teeth jut out over its top jaw.

▲ This crocodile is lying very still under the water. It listens for splashing and watches for movement.

▲ The bottom teeth of a caiman (above) and an alligator are hidden when their mouths are closed.

11

◀ All snakes can stretch their jaws to swallow animals bigger than their heads.

Scaly Snakes

Snakes have scales to protect their skin from the rough ground or sharp rocks as they slither along. Because they do not have eyelids, their eyes are protected by see-through scales. When a snake grows too big for its scaly skin, it just wriggles out of it. A new skin is always growing underneath. Young snakes grow fast, so they change their skin about four times a year.

12

▼ A snake breaks the old skin around its nose by rubbing it against something rough, like a rock. The skin peels backwards.

All snakes eat other animals, from snails to mammals.

blink and seem to stare

A chameleon's tongue

Chameleons

Chameleon feet grip, like hands, onto branches.

A chameleon hides from its predators by changing the color of its body. In the day, it matches the plants and rocks around it. At night, it turns pale and stays very still, like a leaf on a twig. Chameleons can make one eye look one way while the other is looking another way. This helps them to spot predators coming from different directions. It also helps them find insects to eat.

is as long as its body

▼ Male Knysna dwarf chameleons warn off other males by changing from all-green into bright patterns of different colors.

▲ This chameleon extends its long, very sticky tongue to catch food in the next tree.

◀ A basilisk lizard has scaly fringes on the toes of its back feet that allow it to run on water.

Lizards with Frills

Lizards have many tricks to keep themselves alive. Some open a frill of scaly skin around their necks to make them look much bigger. Others have bright blue tongues that they stick out to scare off predators. Lizards are also very good runners and climbers. They have strong legs and rough scales on their feet to help them grip. Some lizards have such hard or spiky scales that if predators do catch them, they are very difficult to eat.

When threatened, the Australian frilled lizard can run on its two back legs.

◄A frightened Australian frilled lizard pops out its frill, opens its mouth wide, hisses loudly and thrashes its long tail about.

▼A male anole lizard stretches out its colorful frill, called a dewlap, to scare off other males.

17

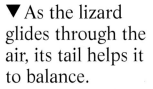

▼ As the lizard glides through the air, its tail helps it to balance.

Flying Lizards

Flying lizards have flaps of scaly skin attached to the sides of their bodies. When they leap into the air, the flaps open out like wings, and the lizards can glide from tree to tree, or to the ground. All flying lizards live in southeastern Asia and the East Indies. Some lizards that do not have these flaps of skin can also jump from trees. They slow their fall by bending their bodies, which act like parachutes.

▶ The flying dragon climbs well but glides to get from one tree to another.

▼ Ribs that stretch out give this lizard bigger "wings."

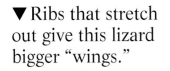

▲ A flying gecko has webbed feet and a fringed tail to help it glide.

Are these lizards really flying?

19

Living in Trees

Snakes that live in trees have bodies built for climbing and clinging. They are usually very long and thin so they can wind their way through branches. Sometimes they also have a ridge along their bellies for gripping onto twigs and rough bark. A few tree snakes can glide between trees by curving their bellies to make a kind of parachute. Most tree snakes are green or brown to match the rainforests where they live.

◄ This blunt-headed tree snake is poisonous. It comes out only at night and eats other cold-blooded animals, like lizards.

rainforest trees

▲ Green tree pythons are yellow or brown when they hatch. They will turn green by the time they are three years old.

Some snakes can go without food for more than a year.

21

Scaly Mammals

Mammals are animals that have warm blood and feed their young with milk. Some mammals have scaly tails and others have scaly feet. The only mammal with body scales is the pangolin. Its scales protect it from predators, and from the ants and termites it eats. To keep ants from biting and crawling into its eyes and nostrils when it is feeding, a pangolin has thick lids that cover its eyes and special muscles that close its nostrils. Pangolins have no teeth. Their sticky tongues drag food straight down to their muscular stomachs.

▶ If attacked, a pangolin protects its soft underside by curling into a tight, hard ball.

Pangolins give off a bad smell to get rid of enemies.

A pangolin's tongue is

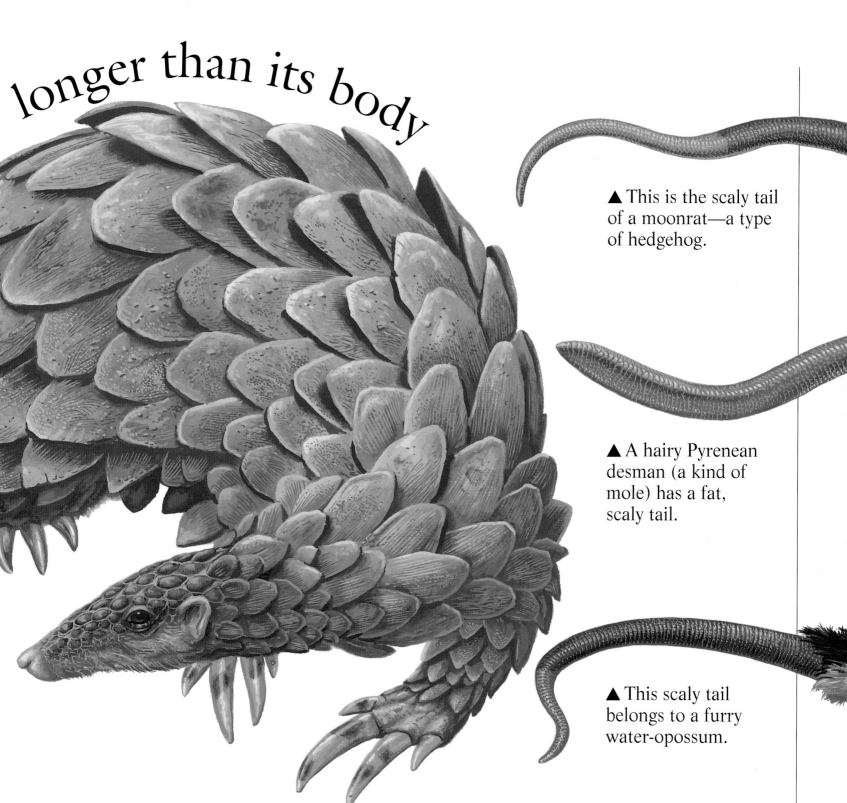

▲ This is the scaly tail of a moonrat—a type of hedgehog.

▲ A hairy Pyrenean desman (a kind of mole) has a fat, scaly tail.

▲ This scaly tail belongs to a furry water-opossum.

23

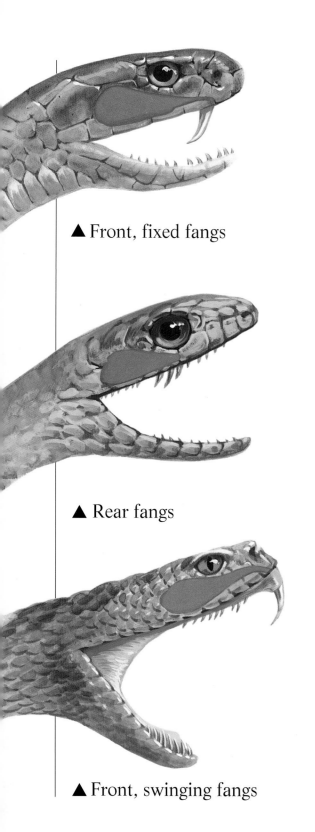

▲ Front, fixed fangs

▲ Rear fangs

▲ Front, swinging fangs

Venomous Snakes

Some snakes squeeze their prey to death. Other snakes kill their prey with poison, known as venom, which comes out of long, hollow teeth called fangs. Venomous snakes have different kinds of fangs and different kinds of venom. Some venom affects the nerves and stops the heart. Some destroys the muscles so the animal cannot run. A few snakes have venom that softens the flesh of the killed animal so it is easier to eat.

◀ Most snakes have fangs in the front of their mouths, but some have fangs at the back. A few have fangs that fold up and swing down.

24

► A spitting cobra squirts venom to protect itself. Cobras also flatten their necks to look fierce.

◄ A rattlesnake has very long fangs to inject venom deep into its prey.

Some cobras play dead when they are in danger.

▲ The moonfish has small, smooth scales and soft fins.

Colorful Fish

The color of a fish is not in its scales, but in the skin underneath. The scales protect the skin, but are almost clear, so the colors can show through. When the sun shines on the silvery scales of some fish, their colors seem to change. Most fish have scales that are curved and smooth, or curved with sharp edges. Other kinds of fish, like sharks, have very sharp, pointy scales.

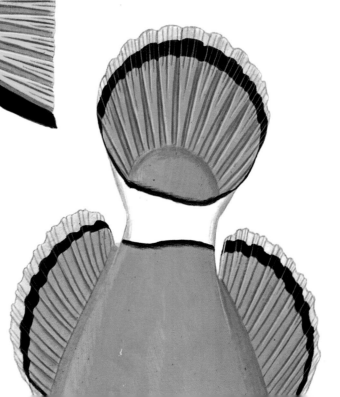

◀ The tiny clownfish has scales with sharp, serrated edges, like little knives.

▲ The surgeonfish paddles with its fins and steers with its tail.

Even when fish are resting, many keep moving their fins so they stay in the same place.

▶The male piranha lets out a scent from its tail to attract females.

▼Australian rainbow cale are all the colors of the water plants they eat.

27

Scales Underwater

A few scaly animals live underwater. Their bodies are perfectly suited to this kind of world. The tails of sea snakes work like oars to help them paddle. They eat fish and fish eggs, and either dive deep to find their food or drift with the tide. They live mostly in warm waters. Softshell turtles also live in water. They hide from enemies and catch fish and insects in the mud on the bottom of rivers and ponds.

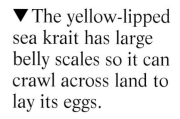

▼ The yellow-lipped sea krait has large belly scales so it can crawl across land to lay its eggs.

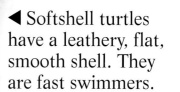

◄ Softshell turtles have a leathery, flat, smooth shell. They are fast swimmers.

28

▼ The yellow-bellied sea snake stays at sea all its life. It gives birth to babies in the water, rather than laying eggs.

Which is bigger, a sea snake's tail or its head?

Life Underground

Worm lizards spend nearly all their time underground. Most of them are legless and tunnel through the ground like worms. They dig with their head, which is toughened with thick scales. The way they dig depends on the shape of their head. Worm lizards have no ears and their eyes are covered with clear skin to protect them from dirt. Unlike worms, they have large, sharp teeth to crush insects.

▶ This spade-headed worm lizard has one big, thick scale on its head. It uses this like a spade to dig through soil.

► Shovel or spade heads push forward and then up.

► Chisel heads turn their heads as they push.

► Keel heads push forward, then to the side.

► Round heads push forward and can turn in any direction.

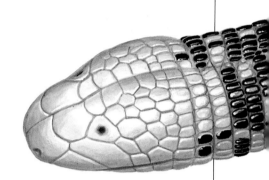

31

Other titles in the series:

Illustrators

(t=top, b=bottom, l=left, r=right, c=center, F=front cover,
B=back cover)

Simone End, 12/13c, 19tr, 28bl, 32. Christer Eriksson, F, 16/17c,
25tl. John Francis/Bernard Thornton Artists, UK, 6bl, 24l.
David Kirshner, 2, 3bl, 4bl, 4/5c, 5tr, 6/7bc, 7tc, 7tr, 8tl, 9bl,
10/11c, 11r, 15bc, 16tl, 17br, 18/19c, 20bl, 25r, 26tl, 26cl,
26bc, 27bc, 27tr, 28/29, 30/31bc, 31t. Frank Knight, 20/21c.
James McKinnon, 1, 22/23c, 23r. Colin Newman/Bernard Thornton
Artists, UK, 14/15t. Trevor Ruth, 3tr, 9tc, 12tl. Thomas Trojer, B.